KATY

C000002055

The Oberon Book of

COMIC
MONOLOGUES
FOR WOMEN

Volume 2

Foreword by
Sharon Horgan

OBERON BOOKS
LONDON

WWW.OBERONBOOKS.COM

First published in 2015 by Oberon Books Ltd
521 Caledonian Road, London N7 9RH
Tel: +44 (0) 20 7607 3637 / Fax: +44 (0) 20 7607 3629
e-mail: info@oberonbooks.com
www.oberonbooks.com

A catalogue record for this book is available from the British Library.

PB ISBN: 978-1-78319-923-5
E ISBN: 978-1-78319-924-2

Cover design by James Illman

Printed, bound and converted
by CPI Group (UK) Ltd, Croydon, CR0 4YY.

Visit www.oberonbooks.com to read more about all our books and
to buy them. You will also find features, author interviews and
news of any author events, and you can sign up for e-newsletters so
that you're always first to hear about our new releases.

Acknowledgements

Many thanks to everyone at Oberon for being so
wonderfully supportive and great to work with.
Thanks to Lily Williams, Charlie Weedon
and Jeanette Hunter. A big thank you to
Sharon Horgan and thank you very much Mandy Wix.

Contents

FOREWORD

Katy Wix makes me laugh 97% more than most people. And although comedy and what you find funny is incredibly subjective, she is the perfect person to have written a collection like this. She's smart but off the wall. She's bold but irreverent. Her voice is unique.

A book like this is long overdue – a compilation of hilarious, sharp, witty and diverse comic speeches for women. So now you don't ever have to go looking for monologues again! No more trawling through screenplays and scripts on the dusty old Internet. She's done the work for you. It's all here! And all of the characters are warm, interesting and very funny. They are a pleasure to read and will be a pleasure to perform.

So have fun. Katy would want it that way.

Sharon Horgan
September 2015

INTRODUCTION

Hello and welcome to the second volume of comic monologues for women you lucky thing! Here we are again. Sure as night follows day, so book two follows on from book one, as I bring you a brand new batch of original speeches.

There are many great books on the market providing audition material for performers, but I was surprised to find that there wasn't a collection of original and contemporary comic monologues solely for women and so decided to start writing them myself.

Naturally and correctly, everyone is now bored to the point of menstruation with the joyless and hopefully moribund 'Are Women Funny?' debate. To me, the idea of asking if something is funny is like saying 'What's tasty?' Humour is surely as personal as your shadow or hairstyle. Wait, hang on – I wasn't even going to engage with it as a debate. Oh balls, right, that's enough of that.

Like most overdone monologues, they are overdone for a reason: because they are good. However, the more performers I spoke to, especially those who wanted to perform comedy and enjoy performing something unheard, it became apparent that there was a real dearth of contemporary comic content. The classics remain a staple diet for any actress, but when it comes to comedy it seems they are subsisting on more meagre portions, which is why I wanted to write a second volume.

A monologue is often the point in a play where the character *must* speak; an impulse which summons them to voice something. And yet I read a great many speeches where female characters were either assuming the role of caretaker or rather helplessly reacting to events in the plot rather than actively changing them. There was a sense of passivity – an external rather than internal locus of control. Let's give them the umbrella title for now of the 'Why Doesn't He Text Me Back? What's Wrong With Me?' monologues. Self-critiquing and being a loser in love are of course British comedy staples, but I didn't want it to be the only way of getting a laugh. If there were a Bechdel test equivalent for anthologies of original comic monologues for women then I like to think that this book would pass.

A lovely young actor called Megan very kindly took the time to write to me and phrased it perfectly:

'As a 6ft tall "definitely not a Juliet" actress you have no idea how refreshing it was to find and read your incredible set of real women who also happen to be unbelievably hilarious ... also thank you for creating women who are able to talk about things other than men ... very rare and very appreciated.'

A NOTE FOR PERFORMERS

Ordinarily when preparing an audition speech it is necessary to read the full play to better understand the character and situation. These monologues exist in a vacuum – if you will – free of contextual restraint. I have deliberately not included a playing range or accent. I would encourage you, the performer, to feel free to create your own story and background to these speeches and decide on your own interpretation. They are designed as a vehicle for you to best show off your performance skills.

I hope you find a speech that makes you laugh and that you will enjoy performing.

Good luck!

Katy

AN UNPLEASANT EVENT

I was seven when I saw my first trapeze artist die.

Not ideal. I say 'my first'; it was my last as well. Haven't got the stats. Not sure how many trapeze artists are scooped up off the floor at the end of a show say, in a year. I don't have the figures. I've only witnessed the one, as I say, I'm sure there's been others but you know, well, if a tree falls in a forest and all that. Oh yeah, she fell alright, but this wasn't a forest, it was a tent … And it wasn't a tree, it was a woman. Splattered like an ink splodge, sequins everywhere. Never forget it. Even the elephants looked up – and they'll never forget it and not just because they're elephants. 'Zut Alors', I thought to myself … if I'd been French … but I'm not. Lovely pink tights she was wearing. Absolutely spot on. She popped herself on the ladder and she had a good old climb. Reached the top – quick smile to the front row and she was off, like a little snowflake floating on the breath of a dream, beautiful and absolutely no hint of the death to follow. Until the tragic death, it was a ten. She began to build momentum; back 2, 3, 4, forward 2, 3, 4. She unfurled one pink leg, slowly, teasingly as if it was trying to tell us something.

I was transfixed. She looked like an Alison, if I was to have a stab. But I often think people are called Alison and I'm nearly always wrong apart from the time I met Alison Gatt. I thought, 'Hello, she looks like an Alison' and I was a hundred per cent correct on that occasion. She's dead now too. But she died, naturally … I mean she died in the nude. But they stuck a dress on her for the funeral, of course;

catholic, open casket, you see. Gawd: two Alisons, well, a suspected and a confirmed one, both dead and what's the connection? Moi. What's the common denominator there? Keep up, it's not hard ... me, is the answer. It's me.

The bar, she just missed the bar. It was a bar-related death. Well, it's an odd thing to want to do isn't it? Have you seen those bars? They're tiny.

D'you know who I feel sorry for, in all of this? The clowns. Imagine that. You're dressed up like a bell end. You've committed to all that (*gestures her own face*) I mean, clearly I feel sorry for the faller, but c'mon – those clowns! They came running on and well, they tried to look sullen but, you know – there was no disguising those painted-on smiles unfortunately.

I hope it wasn't suicide. I never thought of that. Just hadn't occurred to me ... god that's horrible.

The ringmaster did sod all. He just gawped from the sidelines. Didn't even seem to know basic first aid. Not sure what the point of ringmasters is to be honest. He can't even prevent a fatality in his own ring. Disgrace.

BOTTLEWASHER

(She looks around.)

Oh very clever! Yes, very clever! Where is it? Come on, what have you done with it? I know you've moved it! Don't give me those cow eyes – you know exactly what I'm talking about. Have you stolen my parcel? I got a text and an email assuring me that the parcel was delivered this morning. And they said that a man, in pyjama bottoms with no dignity, which is clearly you, signed for it. So where is it? I've seen you hanging around the communal hallway. I think there is something sinister going on. Are you fiddling with our mail? There's no money in there – we're all broke, you know. The others said that I shouldn't confront you, that I should write you a note in case you were scary, but I'm not scared of you. I don't know how you've done it, don't care, just give me my parcel please. Probably illegal anyway, what you've done. You're not allowed to tamper with the mail. I need my package urgently please and I will be really pissed off if I don't get it today. It could be a kidney, for all you know – how do you know that this parcel isn't important? Obviously, it's not a kidney but you understand my point. Tampering with her Maj's Royal Mail, you should be ashamed. I did A-level law mate, I know about this kind of stuff. It is illegal to tamper with post or post boxes – it's criminal damage. I'm not kidding mate – a 51-year-old man got arrested last year when he spray-painted a post box gold in honour of the Olympic sailor Ben Ainslie.

Was it you that made the complaint about our music, the other night, saying it was too loud? Was it? You could barely hear it! Right, let me tell you something …

We are a house full of young women, ok – how would you like it if two police officers appeared at the door and accused you of something you hadn't done? It's not very nice, is it? We were just quietly studying. Have you got something against students? I've heard you muttering stuff under your breath a few times as I've passed you in the street.

Well, it's actually very difficult being a student these days. We're all getting into masses of debt, so it's actually a very sedate and studious atmosphere in our house.

About a quarter of graduates after they leave will be unemployed and the ones that do get jobs, well, they'll probably get stuck doing something menial like window cleaning or bottling things. And it's worse for us women because we get paid less than men, so it will take me even longer to pay off my loan.

So come on – hand it over.

BOUNCER

This bouncer guy drove me back from the bar. He was a genuine guy, dead nice and Greek, just on his father's side. He came around to open my door for me, which I thought was sweet, but a little creepy at the same time. He might have winked, but I'm not sure. It could have been the wind in his eye. We drove through the city at night, which I never normally do. Well, I can't drive. That's the only bit of the job that I like – seeing the city in the dark, but sober. You see and hear a lot when you're sober, don't you? I like it. I think I actually prefer being sober now to the rag-dolly Anna drunkenness. It was easy to talk to him. A city can really gobble you up can't it and spit you out again if you're not careful. I could tell that he understood that.

It was nice to be able to chat to another outsider I suppose. He was from somewhere else too. What's being a bouncer like then I asked. This took him by surprise a bit I think – like no one had ever asked him for a review. He said, 'It's shit and you have to stand outside'. I laughed a big gurggly laugh because I hate working in that place too. My feet hurt, my back hurts. It's a crappy job, a really crappy job. The guy that runs it is obsessed with fusion cooking. Fusion cooking! He wears a little bead on a choker round his neck and all the food and drink has to be a fusion of something with something – it's relentless. Maybe he was spoilt as a child – doesn't like to choose – wants everything. Or maybe he's just a prick. We really bonded over what a, yeah, I'll go with prick, he actually is. Just always shouting at everyone and strutting about like a pigeon in a choker.

He asked me what I really, really wanted to be deep down and I just thought 'Oh deary oh leary, I'm too embarrassed to say' but then he said he'd tell me his if I told him mine! So we count to three and this happens: me: Actress – (obvs). Him: accountant.

Oh, I say – how … I mean … how, well, I thought people probably just fell into accountancy, just a day job, rather than having a burning pash to be one.

Theory sunk.

There was quite a long silence and then he said, 'No offence but …' and when someone says no offence but, you know it's going to end in tears.

'No offence, but – acting looks quite easy – it's just talking isn't it?'

I didn't like that.

Actually, I said – it takes a lot of concentration and effort – acting.

Acting for the camera is like being in the same room as a person you are secretly in love with.

When we got to my house, he got out and opened the door for me.

Do you mind if I follow you on Twitter, he said. I'll think about it, I said.

BRIAN

(She is texting.)

Frothy cappuccino, ice-cold beer and crisps. There. I've texted Brian.

He might be on his way *back* from the buffet car now of course, but hopefully, God willing – he got the message at the critical time. So, let's just see …

I mean, you can't just have blueberries for lunch, can you!?

Yes, all we can do now is just sit back and see what Brian appears with, really.

He's attached to his phone, isn't he, Brian. I can't exactly imagine a scenario whereby he *hasn't* seen the message, and we did say, didn't we – that we'd text if we'd changed our minds and felt peckish – we said we'd text through an order, which we have done. Totally attached to it, isn't he … that phone … especially now his depression is back, don't you think? He's on it twice as much. It's a sort of retreat from people, isn't it?

(She looks out of window at view.)

This is nice! This is nice! Where's this then? Very nice.

I hope we make up the time. We left about ten minutes late didn't we?

(She tuts.)

What this country lacks in a reliable rail network, it certainly makes up for in stunning views.

Mm, picture postcard perfect isn't it? Better than looking at yourself anyway.

Iron I think it is! Or it could be Vit D? Anyway, one of those – I don't have enough of, which means I'm very pale. I don't like to look at myself.

I'd kill for sunburn. Kill. D'you get vitamin F? It certainly doesn't go all the way up to Z, I know that much. Good Trivial Pursuit question that: how many vitamins are there?

Oh come on Brian! Some of us are lacking in essential nutrients here!

(She laughs at little at this.)

I'd kill for a frothy coffee. Kill. And I mean that. Haha, well maybe not kill a person, but an animal perhaps, mm, no actually. I'd kill an egg. I'd kill an egg for a frothy coffee.

I actually score very low down on the psychopathic scale; low thirties. Well, I'm so tired all the time …

I hope he doesn't come back with just water! Water is so boring. Don't you think water is just so boring? Water is just absolute death to me!

I had this unbelievable thing happen to me once …

(She carries on staring out of window.)

Yeah …

Can't believe how calmly I took it actually …

(Realising.)

Oh sorry – I haven't said what the thing was, have I?

I saw a gold bug.

This was only a couple of weeks ago. I'd upgraded to first – weekend upgrade mind – only fifteen pounds – feel special for a few hours – unlimited, to a point, teas and coffees –

speaking of which – has Brian been pushed from the train or something, haha!? Anyway, I'd just sat down, reached into my bag for my laptop, when this golden bug just marched across my hand. It wasn't a bee. It wasn't a wasp. It wasn't a hornet. It wasn't a moth. It wasn't a leaf! It certainly wasn't a mayfly or a mosquito. This was Cumbria, remember – so what's a mosquito doing there?

Wasn't an aphid. Wasn't a midge, wasn't some bulging gnat, wasn't a pea weevil. What was it? It was nothing! Nothing I'd ever seen before, at least. Inspector came round, did his thing, I looked back and the bug was gone. I was stressed at the time, but you know it was as real as the mustard in your sandwich.

Oh good – Brian's back! Oh … oh … with an expression that screams I am without the frothy coffee!!

BULLDOZER

I've really missed you this past week. I kept turning around and expecting to see you there like a shadow! I didn't mean to insult you. I just meant that I couldn't imagine you camping. If I had known, well, how it was going to be received, I certainly wouldn't have said it. I only meant that, well, you're urban aren't you? You like wearing black and a lot of mascara. But not too much! I think you wear just the right amount of mascara – for you – for your face – which is lucky because you have your face.

Let's not have a fight. Come on! I could tell from ten paces away that you were in a mood. So, I can't imagine you camping and I think you wear too much mascara, who cares what I think?! Haha.

Christ knows what you think of me!? Haha, you probably slag me off all the time!? You don't do you? No! Don't answer that. If you can't slag off your best friend, you know then, well, that's – well, that's not democracy. But I bet you do …

You probably think, well, it no doubt annoys you that I'm always going on expensive holidays. I'm sure that's true. It must jar to see one's friends so well. I can't help it if my dad is supremely good with numbers. Yes, I know, we always used to holiday together, but we're too old for that now – perhaps that makes it all the more harder to bear, I don't know.

You can't be jealous of my nose! HAHA. It's like a conch! But, you have to admit – I do have a terrific sense of smell, and an old boyfriend once described it as majestic! Turns out he was right … no, literally, I mean – daddy recently found out that we're direct descendants of The House of Lancaster. You remember from school – the Plantagenets and all that mob, Henry III. We did do it. Oh maybe that's when you had glandular fever. Oh my god – shall we get really drunk tonight!? I haven't done that in ages. I know what you're like … hollow legs, I can't keep up with you though – you're like a massive container. That's another reason to hate me! You're always doing really healthy things and I do literally nothing but people still think I, like, make this huge effort to stay healthy, which is really weird. I'm like an Olsen twin – in every photo of them, they are just munching on junk food. How do they stay in shape!?

So, how *was* the camping trip? I just can't imagine you hammering in tent pegs with your – and you'd be the first to agree here – famously weak wrists. And as for you and creepy-crawlies: lots of opportunities for hysterics there, I should imagine! Oh dear. No, I just can't see it, I'm afraid.

CAMEL

Aw, no, that's my old email. You wanna get my DJ address. You got a pen, yeah? Ok, so it's djbassbump, all little letters, but it's an underscore between 'bass' and 'bump' @hotmail. co.uk. Cool, so yeah, just basically I can do whatever you want, I can play big rooms. I can play small rooms. The important thing is, I can really get a crowd moving, you know. So, as soon as my manager gets out of prison, I'll get him to call you. They can only hold him for 24 hours, so it will either be tomorrow or the day after, but he'll defo call you and then we can talk numbers, yeah. He's been stalking someone, his ex-wife I think, and they gotta lock him up overnight, so he can like, contemplate. But he's a really top guy.

I'm not gonna lie: Tuesday nights are slow. I dunno if you're gunna get big numbers, but we could always just lie and say it's a Thursday and hope people don't notice, you know.

But I'll get the word out, that there's an event going down … see, there are a lot of misconceptions about DJs, okay. People think it's easy. But let me tell you, as a DJ, you gotta be your own producer, mixer, promoter … you gotta do the lot. I'm pushing the name all the time, you know 'DJ Bass Bump'. I don't ever have a day off.

And especially being a girl – not many of us around. But, like I always say to people, 'Ears are blind!' you know? 'Ears are blind.' You come to one of my nights, you listen; you tell me. And I'll ask you, 'Was that a girl or a boy?' up there tonight and you'll be like, 'I don't care, but whoever it was, IT WAS SIC!' That's the main thing. I play originals too.

Not everyone does that. Like people can be so judgemental: the other day, I was in a petrol station and I had all my hair scraped back and I'm in this little velour tracksuit and I swear the security guard starts following me around and he's watching me pick up the cornflakes, so then, when I'm at the till, I give them loads of pennies instead of breaking into a fiver, which really annoyed them.

D'you know DJ Dead Camel? Well, we were at a club last week and he complimented me on my track selection and I nearly lost my mind! He's where I wanna be in five years time, he's a real artist you know and he's got half a beard, it's like his thing and now everyone's doing the whole half a beard thing. He told me that he was DJing for top fashion shows as well for extra money and that he gets ten percent off beach wear. He's really cool. So when people try and come with a comment, just because I'm a girl, I'm like 'Don't come with a comment, cos DJ Dead Camel has got my back'.

Ok, so, I'll see you on Tuesday, yeah. Also, I don't do requests.

Cool, cool. Oh also, do you have like some kitchen towel? I just noticed I got toothpaste on my top from this morning. Oh and can you make sure you spell my name right on the flyer? Cool cheers.

COMMUNION

Dear God, I know I haven't really spoken to you since I was a little bud, but I didn't have a credit card bill as long as a novel back then, did I? Are you punishing me for being in so much debt? Is it a sin? Do you find the use of credit cards insulting because it denies *you* the opportunity to provide, is that it? Well, if borrowing money goes against your Commandments, then you need to spell that out more clearly.

Job-wise, it's not looking good. Why didn't you intervene at NatWest when they agreed to give me the stupid card? Why didn't you make a burning bush appear in the middle of the branch or something? Perhaps suffering is part of your higher plan for me. But God, if I could just get this job, if I could get this job today, then I promise that I will never, ever ask anything from you again. I swear. Can I just have this one thing and then I'll shut up. That's all I want. Just a little job and I'll give a huge sum of money to charity, actually, no, I can't afford to do that. I'll do random acts of kindness every day, for a month. I'll move the cartons of milk with the marginally later sell-by dates to the front for the other shoppers to see. I'll even carry extra umbrellas just in case I see a stranger getting drenched and I'll hand out socks to the homeless and write five-star reviews, at random, on Amazon.

Being alive is difficult. I just need this job today. You owe me one, God. Without your help, there's no way in hell I'm going to get it. Sorry, just then when I mentioned hell – I didn't mean to make you uncomfortable. All I'm saying is – it will take a miracle to get hired, and you're quite well known for doing miracles aren't you, that's kind of your thing, hence why I'm talking to you now, boss.

Ok, God, if you heard all that then please send me a sign …

Pause.

God, did I ever tell you that I once saw the face of the Virgin Mary in 27 kilos of Cheddar?

Just do something like that again …

Pause.

Ok, well no pressure. You can just send a sign in your own time.

There must be people out there worse off than me, who deserve less? I just need to get this job. I can't get into any more debt, you see. You won't let that happen, will you though? Don't let that happen. Don't, don't, don't.

Honestly, I will be a changed person: cautious, careful, easy and pleasant.

I hope you understand – this was a big deal for me today. I don't usually like asking for help, so you know …

I feel vulnerable. Feel like I'm on sand. I could sink any minute. Nothing is solid. I just need to get this job. So, I'll leave it with you, yeah?

COUNTRY MATTERS

Excuse me, but I don't agree and I would like to say something.

You say that, 'Semiotically, I am not an English rose' and therefore not suited to the part, but I think that is erroneous and out-of-date.

I have seen Hamlet, 'the student Prince' played by chubby men in their mid- to late-thirties, so I actually think it's very sexist what you've said. I think I would make an excellent Ophelia, because she, like me, was also a victim of patriarchy.

Do you think that the audience won't believe that our own Hamlet would believably fall for me, that the audience will be giving each other a sly nudge in the stalls and whispering 'She's not in Hamlet's league'?

Because, attraction is a lot more than just looks, you know. Despite the fact that Ophelia is, and let's be honest here, rather one-dimensional, compared to ol' Ham, I'd still rather hang out with her than him any night of the week. Never mind how pure or naive she is, at least she's not a boring narcissist like Hamlet. He probably doesn't even care about what she looks like. He's only going out with her because she's attentive to his every need.

My looks may not be routinely dazzling but, if we are to believe the old adage that 'beauty is truth, truth beauty', accepting the fact that I look like most women and therefore am 'real', I must also be truthful, ergo, I am beautiful.

And my beauty is free of prejudice.

Also, not to put too fine a point on it, but I would have thought the most important thing you need is someone who can act, and that I can do! If you're looking for a living, breathing, unpredictable and complex Ophelia, then you've come to the right girl.

Well, that's my feeling. I bet I'm fired. I'm fired aren't I?

Well, I am anxious to know your opinion. Do you agree?

CREDIT

I've got to pee. I always need to go pee when I get excited!

So don't *you* piss on my parade! Because I haven't been this excited since … since I found out there was going to be a spin-off of *Breaking Bad* – so I'm going to have to be a little bit protective here.

This is real. This isn't a dream. I've just got a good feeling about it. I'm a great believer in instinct. What else is there? I'm like a hungry rat when it comes to money! Sniff sniff!

You like reason and intelligence and boring things like facts, whereas I respect emotions, senses, impulses and the funny feelings that I get. Have you read *The Secret*? No, actually, you'd hate it, but it's been proven correct now. Even the psychologists agree. You create your own reality. And that's all *I'm* doing – creating our own reality for us, I'm designing it, building and shaping it, like … like a master chocolatier. We're not being victims of our circumstance. This has come along at exactly the right time for you and me and it is going to make us money.

I'll be honest, I know I'm not always, but I have hated this last year – listening to you sigh as you leave for work because you hate your job so much. I wake up in the night thinking we've been robbed and then I remember that we sold all our stuff on eBay. My bum is so offended by the economy loo paper. I found a grey hair last night. I'm young. Well, if that's not stress I don't know what is. Come on! This could be it.

You've always been uncomfortable when I express passion for something. You like it when we act like we're dead on the inside and as if we've already given up.

All we have to do is pay three thousand pounds investment money and then we just have to find eight other people who will invest as well, so that's my sister, both your cousins, me and you, three more and we're sorted. Then, they said that in a few *days*, we will get £23,000 pounds back on our investment! The woman who runs it is like, in her sixties, well spoken and she said she used to be vice president of the Rotary Club. I said that I didn't really know what that was but that it sounded very impressive. She's really nice and said that they were being very selective about who they asked to invest. Yeah.

Oh and she said that it definitely definitely definitely wasn't a pyramid scheme.

CURIO

Well, you know, I took so many drugs that I ended up thinking I was Mary, the Virgin Mary. Yeah, I totally believed it. And life as the Virgin Mary was pretty pretty good. It was no different really, it was just that I was the Madonna and child, but without the child. Like I say, I was tripping, massively, tripping off my face, you know, but this went on for about a week afterwards as well, but it was manageable, you know. I was working in a shop at the time and we sold, like, knick-knacks and what-nots. Gift shop really.

It wasn't a strong dose or anything but I was feeling, maybe a little more receptive than usual. A face appeared to me that looked very much like the Virgin Mary. That floated around a bit and I was just getting comfortable with that and then she spoke and she says:

'You alright?'

and I says, 'Yeah'.

and then she goes, 'You know – you're just like me?'

and I go 'Yeah?'

And she goes, 'Yeah'.

I just thought it was normal, a natural part of reality. Believed she was real, definitely, because my first thought was – oh great, finally – someone wise to talk to – someone who's lived a bit – been around a while.

It was euphoric actually, at the time.

I went home, still high. Went to sleep, woke up the next morning and I thought, 'Oh yeah – I'm the Virgin Mary'. They were a bit freaked out in the shop because I turned up with a blue scarf draped over my head and like I didn't really reference it all day, so they didn't say anything. I think it would've been fine, you know, because it's quite a trendy part of town and I think they just would have thought – oh well, it's probably a new fashion thing or whatever. I made it worse though cos, and I don't totally remember this but I asked my boss for the rest of the week off? And she said, Oh why, are you unwell? And I said, no, I've got to give birth to Jesus.

And of course, I was sent home. Which, looking back, was stupid because I needed the money.

Nothing bad happened, I basically spent the week in a headscarf taking pregnancy tests. I read a bit of the Bible, stuff about the second coming and you know all that stuff about the last judgement and the sea throwing up its dead.

Anyway, it only lasted a few days and then I was back to normal. I wentback to work on the following Monday, back to the gift shop. I walked in, and they'd had a new delivery of novelty Jesus soaps. They weren't selling.

DOLLY

How long have I been a writer? Oo, about …

(She looks at her watch.)

… twenty minutes.

You want to speak to my sister – she's the brainy one really. I'm the one who got the sparkly toys. There's more chance of a rich-tea biscuit going to university my dad used to say – but don't worry because you're a dolly, you're a flower, you're a beauty – you don't need maths when you've got a nice face.

I haven't told my sister I'm here today – I don't know what she'd think. She's the writer really, not me. She was going to come but she's having acupuncture. Now there's a cruel thing, not the acupuncture – I mean nature! She got all the brains, but she's a timid little thing, you know – shit scared of everything, whereas I'm hardly shy – I'll kick off at anything to be honest with you – I'm always on the bounce about something, but I never read the papers – I'm more into *Cosmo*.

The only time I ever took an interest in immigration was when the woman who does my nails got sent back to her own country – I was gutted – for the both of us.

(She looks at her nails and then notices.)

Shit! One of my nails has come off. Shit!

(She starts looking around for it.)

Sorry about this – I'd better find it … shit! They're expensive – Korean – real nail as well, apparently.

(She gives up looking.)

This is the first thing I've ever written … where I've really tried I mean.

I thought, no – I'm not gong to listen to all those negative voices in my head. Arsehole FM I call it! It's like there's an absolute arsehole living inside my head saying:

– You can't write!

– You didn't go to university!

– You didn't even get GCSE R.E. and everyone knows that's the easiest one!

But this time, I turned the dial down a bit, bought a new desk tidy and just sat and wrote.

My dad used to say – there are two types of people in this world: talkers and writers. Your sister's the writer – guess which one you are? But I *love* stories. I thought well, what's the difference? I talk in my head and then I write it down. If you slashed open my head right now and turned me upside down then all these stories would fall out.

(She spots something. She bends down and picks up her nail.)

Oo! Found it!

DROWNING

I was thinking about my daughter. I don't have one. My imaginary daughter I mean, and if I would make a good mother.

The thing is I need help. I can barely look after myself. I owe it to my future daughter to sort my shit out as t'were. Today being a good example – all I've achieved today is eating a strawberry yog. That's all I've done. I sat on that sofa and I ate a strawberry yog.

The problem is … I think I'm addicted to self-help books. Yeah, I'm sure that's it – now I say it out loud. That's the problem. I can't get enough, can't take my eyes off them.

I often find myself standing in the self-help section. They're huge. So many titles and I need them all. Somehow I need them all – every single title could have been written for me. Do you think the term hypochondria also applies to mental health anxieties as well as physical ones? Or perhaps the self-help book obsession is just a symptom of an anxiety disorder?

Am I turning into Woody Allen – that's one of my concerns – one of the things that seems to keep me awake at night at the mo. Too much angst, you know, and then worrying about my worrying and the thinking about my thinking until I think my brain will pop. I try to think of calm seas – I try and breathe like a happy sea – gentle in and out as the waves do.

First it was Buddhism and I learn that life is suffering, but then I read about the law of attraction and that actually life was only bad because you were attracting bad things with your thoughts. But then how can that be – I'm an ignorant piece of shit for even thinking that – someone starving in Africa has brought it upon themselves by having negative thoughts? Hardly!

Connection is key but we should also learn to be independent. Love is the answer but don't be too compassionate or you'll get walked over. Practise gratitude but also know when you're worth more! Think nice thoughts about yourself but don't be in denial! Be in the moment but learn to be responsible and organized. Be grown up but do get in touch with your inner child. Be vulnerable but be assertive. Love yourself but don't be a narcissist. Follow your bliss but don't be so selfish! And it goes on and on and on … and I can't help but notice you've stopped listening.

DRUMS

I was in a band. 6 Music even played one of our songs
a couple of times: *Kookaburra*. It featured the sound of
an actual kookaburra. The rest of the band were totally
sceptical about that, but the track was so depressing and
then, suddenly, out of nowhere, a kookaburra 'laughs' loud
and clear. Surely the irony wouldn't be lost on the listener
that the kookaburra is mocking and laughing at the very
music industry itself. And if someone didn't get that, then
they probably wouldn't appreciate the rest of the album,
which is just called *Album*, incidentally, so if anything it was
a way of phasing out the wrong kind of listener.

Anyway, we did ok, got a bit of press attention – did a
little tour; student unions and arts centres mainly and the
odd, and I do mean odd, music festival on a lonely island
somewhere no one had ever heard of. They used to write
about our look, you know. It *was* awesome – the court of
Louis XIV meets new-rave ... so for example a silk chemise
twinned with a neon whistle.

I was single at the time. I'm not trying to justify it but it
must be hard, you know, to stay faithful, when you're on the
road. There was only one guy in the band, he played bass
and oh my god – we'd come off stage and these hot girls
would just hurl themselves at him. I dunno. It was just so
easy. *They* were so easy and available.

But it doesn't work the other way round. When I came off
stage, I would get these shuffling spoddy weirdos who would
just ask me things like:

'Some drummers angle the hi-toms towards themselves, while others, for example Clem Burke the drummer in Blondie sets them horizontally. Is this just a preference or is this advantageous in any way?'

I'm not kidding.

It's so sexist and unfair.

These girls just see power. If he worked in Asda, it wouldn't be happening, but you put someone on stage for a couple of hours, stick an instrument round their neck that hangs conveniently around their crotch area the whole time and you have a recipe for infidelity and hi-jinx.

I mean it's textbook 'guy in a band' stuff. Tiresome doesn't even cover it. He was so porky and ordinary. I got literally nothing. And weirdly, I get more sexual attention now I work in an office.

EXCHANGE

This isn't working. I'm sorry. It started out ok. The letters were great. You've really helped me with my German, but you're making me look bad – you keep doing the washing-up and *please* put some clothes on! My dad has only just had his pacemaker fitted. As I say, letters were lovely, but now you're actually here, in my house, not working for me mate.

Oh and you know the jig's up, don't you? The jig is up!

You weren't punched by a ghost, on your arm. How do I know? No bruise. I checked. If a ghost had punched you on Monday in Dusseldorf then ergo you would still have a bruise and you don't.

Just put a longer pair of shorts on or something. He has a weak heart my father and he certainly doesn't need to see a young woman displaying her sexual development in front of him, ok? Conversely, *when*, and it's a big if, I come to stay with you and the rest of the Baumgartners in Baden-Wurttemberg, I will definitely not be taking anything off – in fact, I'll be putting more on. Two pairs of trousers for me, yes please!

I want to remember you without bitterness, I really do, so if you could just …

And I don't know if it's the cultural divide, but let's face it – we ran out of things to say to each other on day two. You don't get any of my Simpsons' references. It sucks.

Not sure what I was expecting, but in your letters you just seemed so …

Well, you heavily implied that you smoked and that you'd had sex and neither of these things are true are they? All you've wanted to do since you got here is visit castles, which brings us conveniently onto lie number two: hip hop. You don't have a clue. You clearly adore musicals with all the passion of the midday sun. Really disappointing.

I'm just, I'm really annoyed to bits actually.

I've looked at this from every angle and I feel like I've been catfished quite honestly.

A covenant has been broken here.

I get it – very natural to conceal who one is sometimes. It's not always easy. We're young – we don't know who we are yet.

It's very natural to conceal who we are but well, but nothing. Just put something else on.

EXPERIENCE

Well, you're in for a wonderful treat … because *I* am going to tell *you* the truth. Uh oh! What did she just say!? Yeah, the truth. Sounds scary? Well, it is … n't.

'Truth', defined in the dictionary as 'a proven or verified …', I don't know, I'm making it up, but it's impressive isn't it when people do that – when people throw in a dictionary definition, like when I was in the debating society at school and we employed the same technique, thus winning the argument and, finally, proving that racism was wrong. I think I've misremembered that.

I'll level with you, ok?

Sorry, this is difficult for me.

The truth is, I'm a liar. Or to put it another way; the truth was a lie and I'm not lying. The hypnotherapy wasn't for fear of flying. I actually love flying. I love the fact you can't be contacted. No, my reason for having it was for more … alien abductionry … related … reasons.

Padma (that's my hypnotherapist) told me to be careful about whom I reveal my secret to. I just believe, and have done for some time, that I was probed … well maybe not probed, but tampered with certainly, by hybrid … other beings … I don't have a name for them … sods, haha.

(Pointing upwards.)

That mob!

Yeah. This is serious shit.

And you know how, like, I always come across as a really fearful person – so I jump when the toast pops and I Google sinkholes? Well, this is why. Something happened to me. And now, thanks to my sessions with Padma, I have gone from total despair to just mild depression, which I think is a huge step forward.

It was a Tuesday, about a year ago. I was walking Hope, our beagle, along the canal path when suddenly I was aware of this unbelievable warmth flooding over my entire body – I had to take off my Hogwarts hoody (not mine, borrowed off my sister as I was leaving the house). It was November mind! So that's already weird. I didn't have a watch on – I broke the mechanism on mine when I was doing a wanker sign at George Funnel out of the top window and I must have done it too hard. But I would describe it as dusk. And then I remember seeing something glowing through the darkness and then it got so bright that Hope and I had to cover our eyes. I don't remember anything after that but I came to sitting on the bench with chipped enamel *(she points at her teeth)* and there was slime on Hope's back!

Explain that.

FAME

So … this is what I look like from the front.

(She turns to one side.)

This is what I look like from the side.

(She turns to the other side.)

And this is what I look like from the other side. Get used to it, this is the face you'll be looking at for the next section of your lives. My body is my canvas, no photos please!

But enough about you, more about me.

You'll notice I'm wearing blue which is exactly right for my colouring and skin tone. I'm on the cusp between Capricorn and Cancer, which basically means I'm an asshole. And let me tell you, growing up in Ireland isn't easy. So I didn't. In fact, I've never even been, apart from when I *have* been there – but that was different – I was kidnapped, the ransom? My talent!

Just because I'm standing up here – just because I'm the only one talking right now – don't think I'm any different from you – I still get shit on my shoe just like everyone else. I like the basic things in life – chip shop chips, Zara, 2-in-1 shampoos. I've done it all. I'm real.

Sure, I've looked inside – I've had dark times – wondered who I was and what I've done, and you know what – it turns out there's nothing wrong with me. I'm a legend! And everyone agrees. No need to alter my behaviour in any way.

I'm so tired all the time – you know why? – because glamour never sleeps, that's why!

I try to live every moment as if it were a great blog entry. I don't have a blog but if I did it would be incredible.

When I'm feeing blue, you know what I do – host a BBQ, whatever the weather! I don't care – I'm a maverick. I respect BBQs – it's the oldest form of cooking in humanity – cooking outside. And when life gives you sausages … just keep on expecting more sausages to follow, you know – that's what I've always thought. Life's too short – so what if everything catches on fire – that's what insurance is for. Nothing cheers me up like the smell of laughter and charcoal.

I'll stick anything on there – burgers, fish, pasta – there's nothing that can't be grilled, in my eyes. I once had a lover who grated all his food. It didn't last long.

He dumped me … so I dumped him back and on my birthday too – well two weeks after, but it still hurt.

The best gift I ever got … was the gift of time, other than that – a whole salmon! In the post! Can you believe it!

FIGUREHEAD

I was raised by my grandmother, so no – I never really had that problem – we never used to swap clothes, no. I can't really relate to that, I guess. We were very close though. I think I saved her life. I honestly think, like if she didn't have something to love, she would have died. Like the way that if you give someone in an old people's home a plant to look after, then apparently they live longer, because responsibility is good for us. Well, that was my gran. She lived to ninety-six and I'm sure she lived just for me.

She was a smart woman and a well-dressed woman. Small, all bust if you know what I mean – like she could topple over at any minute. She reminded me of the front of the ship and she was just as strong. Humming, always humming to herself, everywhere she went this low noise, like a wasp, but then after she became ill, the humming was slowly replaced by an array of coughs and gurgles and groans and whimpers. I miss the humming, even now.

I feel really sad when I think about it, because I still had to find a way to rebel – because it's important – that's what young people do, so yes, there were times when I was a little shit, but I was thirteen, fourteen – I didn't know any different.

I was just a kid. She called out to me in the night once and I opened my eyes into the blackness and I heard it, but I didn't go. I don't know why. Maybe, because … I just needed a break from having to look after her. Because when I got to about twelve, we swapped. She couldn't really look after me any more and it was my turn to look after her.

Have you ever seen *Grandpa In My Pocket*?

So, the Grandpa has a magical shrinking cap, like the caps they wear in *Emmerdale*. But only his grandson knows about the cap. It's a TV show, by the way. When he's got the hat on, he's just four or five inches high and the grandson just pops him into his pocket. And then they do stuff like look for hamsters under the floorboards, all kinds of stuff.

I mean, it's for children, but I accidentally saw it once, when I was absent-mindedly flicking though loads of channels. And then, it was during the holidays and I don't know why but I just started series recording it. And then one day, I was watching it and I realized that I was thinking how stupid and childish it was, which is silly because it's not even for adults, so I was thinking that I hated it but also I had tears rolling down my cheeks at the same time.

It's like a really hugely important relationship between a grandchild and a grandparent, you know, and they don't really make many TV shows about it. Well, that's what I think anyway.

GOOD LUCK

Apparently the average adult takes around twenty swimming lessons to learn how to swim. It took me forty-seven. Should I be worried? I'm just not a physical person. I mean I have a body, obviously.

I worry about so much.

I worry about the ice-caps melting. My thighs. My eyebrows. I'm always irked. But I cannot stand, I cannot stand, I cannot stand, I cannot stand, I cannot stand seeing other girls being insecure. I just want to shake them and tell them what a huge waste of energy it is. I mean, right now for example, I'm worried about what I'm going to eat today because I've had breakfast but nothing since. I'm worried about a comment that I wrote on Facebook earlier that no one has liked yet – it wasn't funny enough and I should delete it. I worry that I'm going to fall and break all my teeth, which is stupid I know, or that the world might end really suddenly. I have nightmares about that one. Sometimes it's an asteroid, which isn't a million miles away from reality, well it is a million miles away actually, well, light years rather than miles but, still, could happen. Or another volcano.

I worry that there's probably a hundred ways to wear a scarf and I only know about four of them.

I worry that I'll drop my phone into water every time I'm near some water. I worry about that all the time. I worry that I spend way too much time practising that I'm on a chat show.

I guess the headline is: I'm a lot of fun, clearly. Five minutes spent with me and you will either feel much better about your own life or you will, like me, disappear down a rabbit hole of existential angst. Good luck.

GRAND

So me, Amy, Tan, Kat, Sarah, Jo, Rachel, Lu and Vi are all sitting around just about to have our lunch when Jenny, Nish, Alison and Alison H come over and Nish says, 'Have you ever seen a thousand pounds, like, in cash?' And we're all like 'Hashtag, what you on about?' So, then Jenny goes – 'I've got a thousand pounds in my pocket, cash – d'you wanna see it?' However, I should just say at this point, as a caveat like, that Jenny once said that she was cousins with Peter Andre, which – quelle surprise – turned out to be a total lie – absolute dog shit – was she his cousin. A few weeks later she spread the rumour that Galaxy bars had actual seals' blood in them. Well, Amy and Tan ended up ringing the number on the side of the Galaxy bars and spoke to a woman in customer services and when we asked her if Galaxy bars contain real seal blood – she was Geordie and I read somewhere that call centres always employ Geordies because they came out top in a poll of Britain's most trustworthy-sounding accents – anyway when we asked the woman, she just laughed and said no, but that they did contain gluten – and I'd rather be dead than eat gluten anyway, so I'm glad that I know that for future ref.

So, at this point, I'm thinking – nothing that comes out of Jenny's mouth is the simple truth. I like her. I really like her. She's fun, but you know when you ask people something but the expression they pull on their face gives a completely different answer to the one they gave? I mean like – if you asked someone if they were OK and they said yes, but you could see on their face that they clearly weren't – that sort of thing. Her face doesn't match what she says. Maybe it's called a micro-expression, there's always a flicker with Jenny, that she is … well, I don't know how to say it … concealing a deeper psychic wound. There's a sadness that she doesn't want anybody to see – so she lies, I think.

Anyway, so then Jenny plunges her sweaty little paw into her fake Prada shoulder bag and pulls out a monkey! Oh, hang on – what's a monkey – oh no – that's £500, isn't …

And pulls out two monkeys! Couldn't believe it.

HONESTY

My earliest memory involves a pushchair, a stuffed purple snake, my mother's ankles and a sore nose. How very Freudian! Or is it Jungian? What was actually happening, I have no idea. I may well have missed out a major detail that would give the other fragments of memory a context. But this is exactly how I remember it. I could have lied. I could have easily conjured up something more impressive or just incredibly 'piss yourself' funny. But, I stopped myself. Note to self – you are getting better at not bullshitting – well done you!

One's first memory is like one's first reality check. Modern philosophy happens to agree with me. If one's first memory becomes a lie then there's nothing to stop every other memory from then on succumbing to hyperbole is there?

I lie a lot. 'Did you', my friends would often affectionately enquire, 'make that last bit up?' That was how the running joke would go. Why do most people lie? I think it is usually for four reasons: the first being that real life is boring, the second reason is because the person in question has something to hide, the third: to protect someone from a hurtful truth, and the final reason stands for the thousands of other reasons why people lie. My reason? The combination of a likeable imagination, the typical attention-span of anyone my age, fatigue, but above all else just the simple urge to keep my audience entertained. If I'm halfway through an anecdote and I see my audience, whether it be a singular person, family pet or a large group, start to flag, then I will just take an all-time favourite ending and tag it on to the end of the story I'm telling. The results are always thrilling. Reaction times vary from person to person, but speaker and listener will always share in the unexpected ending of the story – almost as if the speaker is hearing the story for the first time too. Now what could be a more loving gesture than treating your companion to a convincing well-told lie? My pleasure!

INSTANT

I've told everyone that I've lost my voice, but I haven't … there's only so much conversation I can take …

When you're a vicar's wife, you're expected to get on with everybody, constantly. All I wanted to do tonight was stay in my room, eat wine gums and bury my head in a Maeve Binchey. But I can't do that – I'm expected to chat and be polite, nod and smile and so on. You could say I married the church itself. Before we got married, and I married young, yes, but I was very sure – we both were … of our commitment to each other, but before we married we'd been to a barbeque at John's house and some of the other vicars' wives, most of whom I detest, said – 'Oh, it's like having a second job', and I thought no way! That's not what's happening to me! I've got my own career thanks, you see I always thought that's what my husband liked about me – I wore Doctor Martens and I have the Chinese symbol for happiness on my foot – a tattoo, I mean – I wasn't born with it. At least I was told that's what it means – it could mean 'machine wash only' for all I know. The point is – I was different, quite a rebel and certainly not dowdy … and I'd always had a kind of faith, you know. My faith wavers. That's natural. Sometimes it feels like God and I have a sort of tempestuous relationship like Elizabeth Taylor and Richard Burton.

It's been quite a tiring morning you see. The enormous church building costs so much to run and I thought – well, we should really use these buildings for something other than worship – it was my suggestion to open it up once a fortnight and provide lunch for the homeless. Some of the other wives, the ones I hate but never show it – well, one in particular – said that they were worried that this could be dangerous and what if one of them lashes out and does something violent. Not very Christian, I thought. In fact, what a shitty attitude.

If somebody needs help – you help. My husband says that's the only reason he is here: to meet people's needs. And now, I just feel so silly. I'm out here – pretending that I've lost my voice …

I'm in charge of puddings. I was just boiling the kettle for the instant custard and I was struggling to get them out quickly – I couldn't find a big enough container, you see, so I was just putting the custard in individual bowls and then heating them in the microwave one at a time, but it was quite difficult to keep track of whose was whose. So then this lady got served before another gentleman and the man started shouting and before we knew it – he had taken someone else's custard and then they started fighting – custard everywhere. Well, I just had to leave. One of the wives gave me a look of 'I told you so' like she had the god of hindsight on her side!

KEEP SMILING

(She has a fixed grin throughout.)

Keep smiling. Keep smiling. That's it. You've got to keep smiling. Keep that chin firmly up, my girl.

Damp patch is getting bigger. Keep smiling!

It's starting to smell. Keep smiling.

Oo if you could feel my belly. It's hard with stress – gotta keep smiling. Smile through the tears, that's it.

Damp patch is getting bigger. Smells like a baked potato.

I wrote three letters – one got lost, one got wet and one got swept away. I wrote three letters – gotta keep smiling. I told the council, I told the landlord – damp patch is getting bigger. The ceiling is bowing but I'm not a queen. The ceiling is peeling. The landlord came by. Funny little man. Bright blue aura – first thing I saw. Flannel jacket, flappy and skinny. Hate him. Tit. Gotta keep smiling though! Packet of chips stuck to his lips.

Damp patch is getting bigger I said.

But he hasn't been back. Keep smiling. He only lives down the hill. I'd like to spill his blood! Keep smiling though! He'll be back. Scout's honour he said. When was that now? I've lost count – I'm counting my smiles though.

Oo, it's defo got bigger – smells like a household fart.

Gotta. Keep. Smiling.

Cat's had a hysterectomy. Gotta keep smiling.

I've nothing to eat – only frozen cheese – keep smiling.

I've lost three Twitter followers in as many hours – gotta keep smiling.

The only silver lining I can see is the one on the damp patch. It's quite pretty now I look again. Marble effect. I gotta live with it, not against it. Gotta learn to love it. Learn to smile from within, not without.

When's he coming back then? To fix up the patch? Put a patch on my mind too – with all the worry. That patch needs to be fixed. Bloody landlords. Land of hope and glory. The sensible people never win. I'm sensible. Hasn't got me anywhere. I just keep smiling.

Damp patch is getting bigger.

A LEMON TREE

This is my lemon tree … in a pot.

It takes a little more work but worth it. If I'm honest though – it's more leaves than lemons. Oh well, when life gives you lemon leaves, put them in your G&Ts. That's what I always say – well I say, I always say, but I've never actually said it before. Or you can prune the leaves.

Responsibility is not really a word in my vocabulary. If you'd met me as little as a year ago, you wouldn't have imagined me, out here – lovingly growing lemons, baptising the soil with a watering can. I've never looked after anything before, other than myself, I suppose. I had a dog once, but it went off with someone else. I was only 14 – took it very personally: Jacques Brel's *Ne Me Quitte Pas* could be heard on loop for a fortnight coming from my attic bedroom window, but it provided me with little succour. I thought I saw him again in a lane, next to a broken-down car, but it was just a hefty fox.

I know what you're thinking … 'bit early for lemon trees, this time of year isn't it?' Well, it's always too early for something around here – you can't put a foot right.

This is the warmest, sunniest part of the garden. They're the most sensitive to the cold of all the citrus family – lemon trees. Well, I can relate to that – especially when I went through my bulimic stage – I was cold all the time. It only lasted three months, it was after I saw a thing about it on *Oprah* and rather than it acting as a deterrent, it seemed to plant a seed.

It needs me, this little thing. Warm soil, laying down its roots – I know all about how to keep a little thing alive now – will put me in good stead for the future. Cos everyone needs to know where their beginning is, don't they? And who watered them and found them the warmest patch of soil and so on and so forth. Oh, I sprinkle it with pepper dust as well – to stop the passing dogs … pissing on it.

'You live in the wind, you live in wind' my grandma used to say. I never really got what that meant, but I get it now. I was always up here *(she swirls her arms above her head)* but never down here … *(she sweeps her hands down low)* in the tables and chairs world of everyday life – so quixotic – like air on the move … like the whole world's breathing in and out just for you. I had no roots you see, no sense of what came before me or why. Without curiosity, you will die, she would say. Curiosity is our water and without it we shrivel. If you want people to do anything for you or marry you then all you have to do is be curious and ask them questions about themselves …

(She thinks.)

Oh, I'm sorry … and what do you do?

LIKENESS

I took my earrings out. They made me look too frivolous.

Didn't sleep so well so be kind.

(She positions herself into a pose.)

Like this, yes?

Should I choose a point in the distance and fix my gaze?
Speaking of gaze – I'm so glad you told me, really I am.
I knew there was something else, some *one* else. I knew it.
Suddenly now, it all makes complete sense. I mean, can you
imagine if I'd actually fallen in love with you or something
mad, like that? It all made so much sense when you told
me.

I don't know if you know this, but I have one eyebrow
higher than the other. But if I do this face … then they even
out. Shall I do that face? Do you want that?

There's an argument for lifting my arms up like this … but I
suppose that's asking for trouble. Oh, what happens if I need
the loo, which I will – my bladder goes off like a clock with
a quarter chime.

I'm glad you told me. It's rare for me to be able talk about
fabrics and things like that with men. Knew it was too good
to be true. And the first time we kissed and you were so
obsessed with my bum and now, honestly – I feel like the
gods of hindsight are looking down and laughing at me.

Don't paint my nose too big, will you? Shall I hold
something, for scale? That might help, like a tennis racket or

something? I notice you're using a lot of blue. Are you going though a blue period, like Picasso?

Do you remember that time we followed Rufus Wainwright into a health food shop and we talked to him by the big bowl of strawberries and he told us he was looking for the strawberry of his dreams? He was staring at you. Just think, what could've been. I bet those same gods are laughing at you now. You probably could have shagged Rufus Wainwright, is my point, I guess.

Should I smile? No. No, I want to look arty.

MANDATE

Don't let the bastards get you down. I, for one, intend to stay angry – because the angrier I am, the more of an effing nightmare I am – my bark is equal to my bite. If we all stay angry then we'll be heard by those at the top!

You're pulling that face again. You know sometimes, I swear I can hear you pulling that face, even when we're on the phone. It's a face that screams, 'Oh here we go – here she goes – doing her Russell Brand impression again'.

And I know that you and I are very different, but you don't know what you know. You always say to me that you don't care about politics – but you're vegetarian for god's sake. That's a political act right there. And I know it's because you say you love animals but you're a classic Green Party member without even knowing it. The personal is political, my friend. Our small, day-to-day, 'innocent' acts all amount to something. When you're eating tofu – it's not just a bowl of wobbly grey stuff – it's a statement.

But, oh my god – can you blame young people – can you blame us, when there is so much to think about – so many adverts telling you you're a piece of shit and you won't get laid unless you buy this cream or this car or get a face wax or a bum peel or whatever.

But I don't think young people are apathetic – no, that's just lazy. When you're young you probably care more about things than at any other time in your life – just sometimes, maybe, the wrong things. I think young people just need a helping hand, a way in. Stop. Pulling. That. Face.

Ok, case in point, yeah? Your girlfriend. Like how, and I don't mean this in a bad way at all, but if this makes me a prick, then I'll just take it on the chin and say it anyway – your girlfriend has, well, a bit, a touch of … it's like her head is full of butterflies or something. When I told her that this government didn't just have the political will anymore – they had a mandate, d'you know what she did – she just started talking about 'manbags'. She didn't even know what I was talking about. She just wants to talk about Reiki. The pair of you: you are not in the real tables and chairs world. I am. And I'm trying to change things. I won't to sit by and do nothing as this government, the government that we re-elected, tip people out of their wheelchairs and shit on the most vulnerable.

MOOD

(Sung.)

'And I just can't wait to get you home,

And I just can't wait to see your face,

And I just can't wait to be in your space …

And I …'

Mmm, no, I think that sounds a bit weird. I dunno, to the wrong ears … you know – could sound rude – 'be in your space.' I mean, I suppose it's ok – I mean can a woman be in a man's space … in a rude way I mean … well, I suppose they can but only if it was up the … oh no, no forget it.

How about

(Sung.)

'And I just can't wait to be in your personal space.'

That's probably clearer but less romantic. Although, it's not actually a love song – it's more of an anti-love song.

What about this line:

(Sung.)

'And I just can't wait to get you home …'

See, I'm worried that sounds a bit like I'm a parent talking to my child rather than a lover, do you know what I mean?

No, I think it's fine. I think it's self-explanatory: I want to get him home to be alone with him …

Mmm, it's useful being in a relationship, you know, with my songwriting, you know – it means I have a muse at all times. It's good. Was wondering if I should mention the goosebumps thing, but probably won't – not exactly poetic. Oh, did I not tell you – he has this condition which means he has permanent goosebumps. Yeah, I don't know if it has a name … like everlasting bump, but yeah – he has skin like a cock all year round. Cockerel, I mean, sorry. Our first date was in a Bella Italia and it was boiling and I saw it peeping out from under his shirt. All these goosebumps. Yeah, I mean, it's still just normal goosebumps, obviously – it's not one big goosebump, he's not a complete freak, it's just that it never goes away. But I have to tell you – on certain areas of his body – it's not a problem. It actually is quite an advantage point!

He called me in the middle of the day once, panicked – saying that he had just stared directly into the sun for several minutes and nothing had happened – hadn't even hurt before realising that it was the moon. You know, the way the moon is still visible in the day sometimes. I said, no offence – but anyone can look at the moon, hardly worth mentioning mate. Bless him. I think he was starting to think he had super human powers or something. Hardly, I said – you don't even do the washing-up, so you've got a little way to go till you're a superhuman! No one can stare into the sun – you'd be lucky to have lids! Your eyes would smell of burnt sugar – cook your peepers off. You'd bloody know about it.

He doesn't know I'm writing a song about him – it'll be a nice surprise for our anniversary … it's coming up to about seven now … days, yeah only been a week, but when you know, you know don't you, or think you think you know, when you think you know, at least.

ON STAGE

I wrote a poem about snow – don't worry, I'm not going to do it now. I don't remember it anyway.

I was chosen to go up in front of the whole school and all the parents at the Christmas fundraiser concert. Backstage, there were two girls dressed as Christmas puddings. One of them, the one with more holly, pointed at my face and said 'What's that?'. Then I felt it; wet and it was growing, running from my nose and down onto my mouth. So I touched it and there on my fingers was this cherry-red blood. It must have been the nerves. The pudding twins laughed and my cheeks tingled with shame. How dare they. They were the ones dressed as desserts after all.

Then I heard them call my name. I didn't know what to do. There was a long pause and then Mr Francis repeated it once more. It reminded me of when the babysitter used to let me stay up late and watch *The Sound of Music*. At the concert the man keeps announcing the winner, 'The Von Trapp family …, The Von Trapp family …' but they never appear because they are running from National Socialism. The girl with more cream on top nudges me, and her sprig jabs my arm, 'You're gunna get into so much trouble'. So I took a deep breath and walked onto the stage. The blood was dripping down my front.

Little murmurs and sounds of disgust were now coming from the front row but the lights were so bright that I couldn't see their faces. So I began …

Large white flakes do fall to the ground

Silent and soft upon the mound …

… and so on until I got to the end. I don't remember the last line but I know that I rhymed 'penguin' with 'apron'.

Afterwards Mum was cross because she had made the dress especially. It was cornflour blue, but cornflour isn't blue – it's white. The trim was white – she cut it off the bottom of an old confirmation dress that she found in a skip and sewed it on. But she wasn't happy, when she saw the blood down my front she screamed at me like an injured animal, burst into tears, said sorry, and took me to the café round the corner. I had three different types of ice cream, so it was almost worth it just for that.

OPENING

I used to stare at you from behind a wall. You had a bike. I had chapped lips and a helmet. I was saving up for the bike. I watched you practise and practise for your cycling proficiency test. I too prepared … for heartbreak. He'll get the top mark anyway, I used to think. And you did. You went up in front of the whole class to get your high score. I just got a pencil, because I didn't have a bike.

I used to watch you from behind my wall. How can I get closer to you, I used to wonder. Because I was never close enough. I wanted to eat you up, so that you would always be with me wherever I went.

I didn't have many posters in my room, but I had a small picture of you and I would keep it under my pillow. Sometimes I would fall asleep with the phone on vibrate, resting on my heart, just in case. Waiting for your electronic letters to wake me.

From behind my wall, I could guess your every move, so predictable. First you would complete a ring of the car park, then you would practise taking one hand off without wobbling. Then you would weave in and out of the abandoned trolleys. Next, you would make a U-turn so powerfully that I would have to hold my breath, before heading over to the bins to execute a masterful gear change. Your likeability and bikeability were not mutually exclusive.

I would lay my bobbly grey jumper on the ground like a prayer mat and sit cross-legged until my eye could align with the hole the missing brick had created. Then, I would wait for you to ride into shot like the hero in my very own film. You were all I had. Everyone else made me feel small and pushed my buttons but, with you, there were no buttons – they fell off! Button cutter! Button cutter! That was you. You cut off my buttons and made me feel precious. I could withstand an entire school day as long as we both kept our appointments in that car park.

What would happen, I used to think, if I were to come out from behind my wall? To taste the space around you! You would turn and smile as you saw me approach at long last. And you would take the helmet from my nervous hands before gently placing it on my head, to crown me your queen. And you would gesture towards your handlebars, beckoning me to sit on them so we could 'double-ride' around the car park as one, but then I would point out that it was both illegal and dangerous, affecting the cyclist's ability to see, steer and balance, and in some parts of the country so called 'double-riding' could carry a £2,000 fine. And then you would shrug and cycle off into the distance, alone.

OUT THERE

You know, it's so nice to meet someone my own age at one of these things! Which ones are your parents?

(She looks round.)

Oh, don't tell me – there!

You have the exact same nose. That's adorable.

I feel like we've met before – but I can't quite place you. My dog's very emotionally challenged – so I spend a lot of time walking him around Ruskin Park. Are you one of the skateboarders? No, I'm sorry – that's ridiculous – you don't look the type. I just know I've seen you in an outdoor setting!

Anyway, I'll leave it with you …

Are your parents intrusive at all? Mine have been charting my academic progress pretty much since the day I was born with the sort of enthusiasm that only unhappy people in need of distraction muster. That's my set there: don't be fooled – they're older than they look – they've both had a lot of work done. They remind me of the two Vermeers in our hallway: I walk by them every day and think about their immense age.

May I be bold? Do you think we're all in a sexual crisis? Us, I mean: millennials, dotcom-ers, generation X, all of the above. Young people. Do you agree?

Ah! Rock-climbing! I've just remembered where I know you from – Mile End Climbing Wall. Am I right? I thought so! I never forget a face – actually I do … all the time. I'm better with dogs. Dogs' faces.

As I was saying – I'm sure I can't be the first to have so many ideas so young, but our generation haven't yet grasped the sanctity of fulfilling intimacy. I blame pornography. Gratifying sex must surely consist of more than just the end goal – the journey is just as important: the fine interplay between the purely sensual and the mere sexual, I say mere, but of course there is nothing 'mere' about it. For many, sex is as meaningless as shoving some daffs into a vase and yet for some far-off cultures sex represents the great 'intercourse ' present in all of the universe – the joining and coming apart that exists in all, but this is of course all just a hyposofis

(She struggles to say hypothesis.)

just a hyposofis. Hypofis. Oh for Christ's sake – hypofisis … just a theory.

When I do eventually have sex, I will be absolutely making sure that neither party gets trapped in a reductive idea of what sex should be. Us girls shouldn't feel bad about wanting to be wanted. That's just Oxytocin at work, and cities of love have been built on the stuff!

PATIENCE

I'm woken in the night by these noises. Oh, I'm sure it's nothing … probably just the screaming dead, or similar. At first, each sound struck me with absolute terror, but then I just got used to it.

It's important for me to be able to express these feelings openly with you Doctor. The noises seem to come not from this world. One night, I broke wind with such horsepower that I think I frightened the spirits away. They didn't re-visit for weeks after that. But, last night, they reappeared. Words cannot paint what happened next … but I'll give it a good go.

I'd just finished watching *Location, Location, Location* when I suddenly felt really sleepy, and not just because the show had been about new-builds in Chester. Boring! It was only 9:45 and usually at 9:45 I am far from tranquil. I'm usually full of beans. As I'm making my way up the little stairs to Bedfordshire, I began thinking – surely I'm too young to be going to bed at this time. Anyway, I suddenly caught sight of my face in the bedroom mirror, pale and harmless, when I noticed a cobweb in my hair. I yanked it out with force and it really isn't easy for one with such anxiety to withstand a cobweb in the hair. Where was its maker!? The spider! I'm the sort of person who always assumes the alarm will go off when they walk out of shops. And it did once, for absolutely no reason. Three security men in intimidating livery asked to see my receipt and one of them looked like a young Stalin and well, the whole thing was awful.

I'm sorry, I seem to have gone down an avenue.

I got into bed and naturally, buried my face in an old copy of *Grazia*. I used to keep a stack in the bathroom, but they had gone rather crisp. I was just nodding off when I heard someone sigh, just a simple sigh but it wasn't me and I live alone. It came from right inside the room. My blood curdled, honestly, and well, that was it – I was too frightened to sleep – I stayed up most of the night flicking through articles about how to wear tangerine, that sort of thing.

I was thinking perhaps a sleeping-tablet would help, or perhaps it could be something as simple as too much cheese or Irritable Bowel Syndrome, what do you think? I'm very open to your ideas.

PICK

Please get it right. It's a massive deal. Make a long list, then a short list, treat it like the Baftas. It may seem counterintuitive but you might want to wait until the baby is actually born, so you can see its face before you decide, because if you get this wrong, without sounding alarmist, well … it's tantamount to child abuse. Yeah.

God, how I longed to be a Jess, or a Sarah or even something devastating like Brittney. But when the teachers called out 'Pandora' in the playground, only one person turned their head to see, and that was me. There were no others.

It's been a burden, my whole life, my name. And you may think that a name doesn't really matter, *that* much, but it does! What's even worse is that it didn't even suit me. A Pandora should be elegant, serene. I was fat and shy. It's so much worse, like being an ugly Belle, a quiet Gabby, or a clumsy Grace. Some little girls are desperate to stand out aren't they and be noticed, actively looking for signs of their uniqueness, but that wasn't me – I was desperate not to be seen. There was nothing you could throw over the name Pandora to try and conceal it, no chance of pushing it into a corner and hoping no one would notice. I was furious with my parents for forcing me into the middle of the room for all to see … because they named me Pandora. Nominative determinism. Your name affects your future. Because no one called Gary will ever run the country.

And then, when I got a bit older, the boys would make really lame jokes about my box. Well, by then I knew the myth quite well and I would say, 'Actually, that's a complete misnomer. Pandora opened a *jar*, but it's often mistranslated as a "box", and besides, she only opened it out of curiosity, she didn't mean any harm and anyone else would have done exactly the same, if they had been in her position.'

So, this woman, this poor woman Pandora – created by the gods, has been the victim of victim-blaming. It was Prometheus's fault quite honestly. So there we go – who was really to blame – a man. This defenceless woman has taken all this blame – a disproportionate amount of blame – when really Prometheus started it. All Pandora ever did was open a jar, like Nigella – she has been completely misrepresented.

I don't really know how you get it right, to be honest. Sticking to something biblical is always a safe bet, but not Dorcas … or Jezebel, and you should be fine.

RIVERBED

I never feel the cold. People would say 'Are you cold?' and I would say, 'Never'. Winter couldn't even stop me from playing outside. I hated summer and I longed for the earth to turn dark and cold each year. 'Goth Girl', I heard the girl next door shout over the hedge once. But she had a twisted hip, so I wasn't allowed to be mean back. There'd be steam coming out of people's mouths like they were spray-painting the sky. But nothing much came out of my mouth.

My Mum would drag me to the doctors and say, 'What in God's name is wrong with my child? It's the middle of winter and every time I turn my back, she's taken off her coat'. People would say, 'You can't go out without a coat', so I put on a coat. 'You can't go out without a hat', so I put on a hat. I kept the peace. I'd walk for maybe ten minutes, when I'd have to take them off to breathe and stop.

Then one night I wanted to be alone, so I went to my spot. I knew the best hiding places but the minute you see someone else there, well, it's not a secret hiding place any more, is it? It's ruined and you have to let go, move on and find another hiding place. This was one of those nights – I lost my hiding place.

Behind our house was a river. I was in the cool water, up to my ankles, just looking for stones, the ones like black potatoes. I liked to paint them in bright colours and then sometimes I'd write a name on one too and give it as a present. That's all I had to offer – I was just a child. No matter how crap a present is, if it's given to you by a child with no money and big eyes then you have to love it.

The feeling of going down to the water to find my black potatoes was the best feeling I had in my whole life. And the deep river like a big cold dish. Then I see it: a man and a woman. What are they doing?! Are they? Oh my god – they're taking off their clothes! They are naked and by that I mean – they haven't got any clothes on! He was talking quietly in a murmur punctuated by her soft, short laugh. And suddenly, I'm hot, for the first time in my life, I've got flames just under my skin. Flames. Rushing. Sick. Just so ashamed. So angry that, well, it's so stupid because I was just a kid but I was angry that the adults hadn't seen me – I was there first – angry that they hadn't respected my little patch of the river where the best pebbles are. And the noise grew louder and I thought I would drown in shame. The man looked up. He saw me! Our eyes met. It was like I'd been shot in the stomach. I ran and ran and ran, a panting beast, all the way back to my house.

'Oh, where is your coat?!' my mother yelled through the gaps in my heavy breaths. I tried to explain. I had left it on the riverbank. But, no, wait, let me explain! I had to move, get away. Oh! Adults never listen. They never listen.

I went up to my room, seething. Tomorrow I would go back to the river, for the last time, hope my coat will still be there and say farewell to my hiding place – and to my lost innocence.

SOUTH

I could just see his One Direction keyring peeping out from under his T-shirt, so that's how I knew. We were both at the same bus stop and we both looked up and made eye contact at the same time about three times in about seven minutes. I was waiting for the P4 which goes about every two hours. So, I just said, 'Have you ever seen them live?' He looked confused so I pointed at the keyring. But I could tell then that he was a bit shy, like he didn't expect me to speak. I don't mean like he didn't think I knew how to speak, no, more that he just wasn't expecting such a sassy girl at a bus stop on a Tuesday afternoon in such wet weather. He said no he hadn't and looked at his shoes. Then I remembered my uber fact. So I said, 'Did you know that two of One Direction are actually cousins but they didn't even know – like they only found out last week?'

He said he didn't think that was true. I said 'fool' quietly under my breath to myself, to keep the peace really. But it is true. He's wrong.

He starts trying to find a picture on his phone of when he met them. I really wanted to show off my knowledge so I said that a lot of people don't understand all the aspects of being a Directioner, you know. We've got a reputation for being deadly. People think we're crackers don't they – obsessive. But we just really want them to do well and I don't know about you but I also think it's about being part of a community isn't it – something bigger than yourself. It's a form of spirituality – like how my neighbour does chanting in her front room sometimes. It's communion. Why else would we all wait around for hours on end in the cold just to catch a glimpse of Harry's perfect curls. I just wish their management wouldn't push them so hard – I mean look what happened to Zayn. My friend's dad was in a band in the late eighties and the same thing happened apparently but he ended up in rehab 'cause he was addicted to food.

We stood in silence for a moment. I couldn't tell if it was sexual tension or just tension. And I couldn't tell if he was really looking at me or if he was looking at his reflection behind me.

Then the P12 came and he got on it and in a moment of total sorcery I got on too – even though I wanted the P4. But then it was just really awkward because he sat at the back with some old ladies and there was no room so I had to sit on my own near the front. I got off at the next stop and waited for a P4. Honestly, he gives the fandom a bad rep.

I hope they never split up.

SQUEEZE

Look, this whole thing has been like a film. Not necessarily one that I would rent again but …

It's not like I haven't imagined what it would be like to be with you because I have, believe me. I even fancy your shoes.

You're so clever … not as clever as me *(she laughs a little)* but you know …

Undeniably, we have a connection, a spark. And it's obvious to everyone. A few people have noticed and asked me if anything was going on between us and of course, of course, don't worry – I didn't say anything. I was just breezy and subtly changed the subject by saying something like, 'Where do you stand on the whole Russell Brand, don't bother voting thing' and then they would forget what we were talking about.

I feel as though, and I'm not sure exactly when this started to happen, but I feel as though I know where you are in the room all the time.

Ugh, I'm a little out of my depth here.

This has all been very heightened and I think we both adore the idea of it so much, of being together, but I worry that it's not based in reality. I can't image going around Asda with you, d'you know what I mean? It's all so intense with us. I guess we're both quite intense people.

Well, I think I've always met two types of guys really: those that I'm very physically attracted to and those where you fall in love with someone's mind and I suppose what I'm saying is, and this will sound quite full on but, with you … there are both these things and I guess it overwhelms me a little. But, having said that, I am with someone and I can't break their heart just because we like the idea of being together and I know you respect that.

Maybe you're so perfect that I can't relax with you, maybe that's it. I never see your flaws. And in some ways, maybe if we kill this now, it will be so perfectly preserved and never grow old like Marilyn Monroe's face.

Your hands. God, I love your hands.

I'd only take all my crap out on you anyway eventually! It's best you never know. I won't come down from my pedestal and nor shall you. We can stay up there like a God and Goddess, Shiva and Shakti, immortalised by our love. I said love! I didn't mean to. No one has said the L-word up until this point. I didn't mean to say it.

Perhaps, for this moment only, we are in love.

THE BIG DAY

Thank you. Thank you. Thanks so much.

Um, not very good at public speaking and unfortunately I'm not just saying that, so I'll keep it brief. And I'm sure you'll agree with me when I say that the bride looks absolutely ravenous today, absolutely gorgeous – love the hair – really jazzy! And, she was so worried about – because it's very thin isn't it and in bright sunlight – it can go quite see-through can't it, so I'm just glad that the beautiful hair piece arrived on time – let's hope no one had to sell the hair due to poverty to get it to you here today. Right then, well as chief bridesmaid (it wasn't going to be at all actually, was it? Do you remember? I said no at first because today was meant to be the day that I was going on a sushi-making course, and it was non-refundable but then it got cancelled at the last minute, thankfully).

So what makes a good wedding speech? Well, I honestly didn't have a clue and I've only been to one wedding myself – last year in Cyprus (and it was awful). So, I decided to Google it and according to the internet, a good speech should 'share some funny or touching memories about the bride, honour the bride and groom's relationship and offer up advice and well-wishes as the pair begin their lives together'.

Well, that's quite difficult to write, so I haven't done that, but what I have done is to write a list of all the stories that are too inappropriate to talk about, so – you won't be hearing the following:

– you won't hear about the time we snorted coke and went flat-hunting.

– you won't hear about the time we hid someone's EpiPen, as a joke.

– you won't hear about the time we got off with each other in return for free drinks.

None of that stuff.

And your new husband is sat there – look at him – grinning away like the cat that got the cream, and rightly so. As you know – I didn't like him at first, but now – I get it. Having spent a bit more time with him, I get it now … kinda. It certainly proves that love is blind, I mean, well, no – I just mean it's about making choices that make you happy isn't it, not anyone else, which is great.

And the bride's mother looks stunning today as well. It's actually really sexist that – the way wedding speeches always go on about how the women in the room look. It sort of undermines the compliment anyway doesn't it – when you feel obliged to pay one. Anyway, sorry – the bride's mother really does look lovely. *(To bride)* We were talking earlier actually (when we were waiting for you to put your false hairpiece in) and your Mum was telling me what a difficult birth it was when she had you and about the post-natal depression and everything, and I'm just really, because sometimes – you can pass the depressive gene on in a family can't you – but I'm just really glad that that doesn't seem to be the case, so that's good and here's to any future children being free from mental health issues too!

My own mother smoked all throughout my birth – I'm kidding of course! Just trying to get the funnies in …

(There is a slight disturbance at the back of the room.)

I think there's a dog?

Is that a dog?

How did a dog get in here?

Shall I carry on?

I feel like I'm competing with the dog, now … sorry …

THE PAUSE

No, the reason I'm quiet is because you've been talking for the whole, entire time. Wow! Listen to that!? What is that strange and unfamiliar sound? Could it be ... is it ... it's the sound of MY voice! My God, so that's what I sound like. I can't believe it – can I speak now? May I say something? Is it really *my turn*? Thank you! Well, how wonderful that it's finally my turn! I'm just going to get this done really quickly, don't worry. It will be your turn to speak again in a second I promise. We can go straight back to talking about you any minute. I'm literally talking as fast as I can for you, how's that? To your credit, I'm surprised that you even noticed that I hadn't spoken in quite a while, because, and let's be honest here, I think it's fair to say that I've been listening to your shitty monologues for several years now and not once have you thanked me, acknowledged that I'm a good listener or even asked me questions in return when the shitty monologue comes to an end. Have you ever even stopped to wonder what I'm getting out of this? Don't tell me you're stupid or arrogant enough to think I'm even listening to you anyway. The beginning of one of your monologues is really a signal to me that I can switch off for a few minutes to have a think about what colour I might paint the bedroom or practise some meditation techniques, but I'm certainly not listening. I don't even bother to say anything anymore if you use a word in the wrong context or mispronounce something, which you frequently do. There was one occasion, when you had pen on your face and I just said nothing. I think it's time to end the charade, don't you?

And the weird irony is, despite all the speeches, I'm not sure I really know you. If I was to crack open your skull right now then all this pink, fluffy irrelevant stuff would just fall out. You want to gossip or judge or talk about cupcakes, then whenever we get even a millimetre close to talking about something that is actually anything resembling a feeling, emotion or truth, you just say 'Keep it light!', 'Keep it light!' That's your little mantra. Keep. It. Light.

So, here's the deal: I'll swap you a mouth for an ear.

I often hear the real anger in your voice, but you won't admit it. I know that you hate your job, you hate where you live, you clearly hate your family but all you ever say is 'Keep it light'.

Well, two pretend people cannot have a real relationship. So we shouldn't really mourn this. We have both been fake and fictitious. You created a character that was really fun and palatable, and I created the character of someone that wanted to please people and be a good Samaritan but none of it is that real.

The pretend me and the pretend you have two choices: either we start again or we just end it now because it's a show. We either buy more tickets or we storm out of the auditorium and rip the tickets up. It's up to you, what do you say??

THE WALK

Oh look – a hedgehog with its heart hanging out.

Fascinating. Absolutely fascinating.

(She stares at it for a moment.)

(Looking around.)

It hasn't changed much, this place, well, apart from where it's changed massively. So long since I've been here, I was just a little bud myself, just a kid. Maybe ten. It's funny how when you're a child, you're never entirely ten – you're nearly always 'almost eleven' aren't you?

The well! The well is still the same, such a familiar object, I suppose but, I don't know – I never liked it – always used to give me the willies – and I never looked in it – like the old toothbrush mug in my gran's house, never look in it! There was bound to be something old and scary at the bottom!

We could drop a stone down I suppose, you know – to hear how deep it is. I don't think my arms want to though – look: my fists are clenched! Why is it so scary? Looks different today – like it's yawning.

There was this lady … we used to laugh about her … she was always here. Sue Clinch. She was always in the park. And if you didn't see her, then you would at least hear her – shouting at her dog from behind a hedgerow. She was quite terrifying, and remarkable in that she's the only person I've ever met who sounded like she was snoring when she spoke! She had a little dog on wheels, because its two back legs had given up, or conked out or whatever. You would see her, dragging this thing around the place on a little dog trolley. She was probably about fifty but could have easily passed for a forty-year-old that had just led a really hard life. She smelt of gone-off incense and her hair was, well, just the opposite of what sleek is. One thing she did have going for her was a really memorable jumper that she always wore on her walks. It had the word 'Stockholm' embroidered in bright colours across the front. She loved to tell anyone who would listen, that she had actually bought it in Mombasa and 'wasn't it a topsy-turvy world?' Was she aware that people didn't like her? I'm not sure, looking back, I'm not sure. The dog was alive but you would hardly know it. Even though the back end was moribund there was at least a flicker of life at the front – like the way sometimes a torch would still light up for a few seconds even though you knew the batteries were dead. The dog was so vulnerable; it sort of made me feel sick. Reminded me of the time that I accidently popped a tadpole thinking it a berry – I took to my futon bed for a week with grief. Nature can be very unjust can't it?

THREE

No, you go! Don't worry about me! I'll be fine! No, don't worry – you go! Honestly. You go! I'll be absolutely fine.

I was going to stay in anyway and um … paint a table grey. So, yeah. I've been thinking about doing it for a while now so don't worry. Go! Really. Oprah tweeted a picture of herself a few weeks ago painting her table grey and I just connected with the whole grey table vibe immediately. So, don't give it another moment's thought. Go! Go.

Even though it was my idea to go in the first place, that's fine.

Yeah, you have to sand it down a bit first of course, so plenty for me to be getting on with, prep and so on, in fact – stay out! Because there's lots for me to do, so stay out late if you want.

Watch out for that great big puddle just outside – it's been raining quite heavily today – you probably didn't notice – too busy bonding. Too busy staring into each other's eyes. I'm joking of course. Or am I? You know, I'm not one hundred percent sure myself. I think I feel annoyed – d'you know what I mean? No, I definitely am annoyed. Yeah, I sort of feel annoyed, certainly. Mainly because it was my idea originally to go in the first place. But, if there are only two tickets then, well, yes of course you two should go. I mean you've clearly bonded.

And no one has even noticed my hair! Changed the old mane today, that's right! Not a peep out of you two!

Low-lights, you know – been saving up for a while. But you two go. I'll just be grand grand grand! Looking forward to hearing about it! It's a good job I love this wallpaper so much because I'M STUCK WITH IT ALL NIGHT.

So, the headline is: you kids go have fun and I'll stay and hold the fort. It's going to be happy hour here the moment you leave, trust me.

I stayed in last night on my own too, so you know, but that's fine. It's a good job I get on so well with myself, is all I can say. But don't blame me if you come home and I'm slumped over a freshly painted grey table with a cup of bleach in my hand – I'm joking – I wouldn't want to ruin the cup. I'd drink straight from the bottle! But, you go, that's fine. I'll be ok. Maybe I'll paint the walls grey as well and the cups! And the windows and all the tea towels. When you return from your little sojourn everything will be grey … which is really just a metaphor for my life!

TIME FLIES

No, I'm sorry, but I cannot accept this Christmas jumper from you!

I know you spent a long time choosing it and I'm not questioning your gift-giving abilities – you are ever so good at giving gifts apart from the ashtray you got me when I was twelve. It's not *really* about the gift. Look, this is my clumsy attempt at a protest, yes a protest. You know I've started wearing a mouthguard don't you? At night, for my teeth – to stop them from bumping into each other. It's your fault, hahaha, I'm joking, except the truth isn't actually a million miles away from the joke I just made about it being your fault.

There's no neat way to say this, so prepare yourself for mess! You suffocate me!

I'm sorry, but that's how I feel – strangled. I'm not saying this is totally unique to you. This is what mothers do, I mean, I'm surprised that WHSmiths don't have a 'Happy Smother's Day' range for Smothering Sundays, I really am. But I seriously suspect that you are better at it than most.

I suppose I owe you some examples. Do you recall the time when one too many hearty swings of your golf club had resulted in a busted watch? When I offered to buy you a new one for your birthday, just last week, you agreed that that would be lovely but then you followed me to the shops like the secret police because you didn't trust me to get the right one, then you insisted that I get a ride home with you, but on the way home you were extremely critical: you have never

liked any of my friends or any of my 'choices' as it were
and my therapist says that I have to talk to you about our
relationship and how things should change. And living here,
with you, the un-ending interrogation. Those fake flowers
everywhere that never grow, have started to feel like the
insignia of your dictatorship. I have to do some things for
myself … or this bungalow will be my coffin.

Oh my god – that's me! I'm one of your fake plants! I'm not
growing. I'm like a Pinocchio, little rubbery girl … with no
air or water.

What on God's green earth am I going to do!?

WHAT IS LEFT

(She is upset.)

Great big handfuls of back, is what I see.

A sad body. Fixed my eyes right on it. I wanted to look away.
Feel so stupid, because I was so sure that I was more concrete
than that. Well, I haven't seen myself on film in a long time.
Didn't look like me. It was only about four long seconds.
Silly Facebook video posted by one of the girls.

I know you're always telling me about what your brother
went through in Afghanistan and how I should keep things
in perspective, but fuck me, I looked bad. It wasn't pretty.
They say the camera adds ten pounds, but I think that's only
the really cheap cameras, I don't know, I just always thought
the cheaper the camera is, the worse you look, so I should
take some comfort from that.

Everyone's singing Happy Birthday and then I get up to put
my pressie on the table and I'm ALL BACK, it's like a bank
of flesh, a whole pink shrine to greed …

Like a living, breathing human cake museum, just blobbing
to the music, full of cheap wine …

No wonder actors are all obsessed with how they look.
It forces you to scrutinise yourself like never before. My
hair was so … wide and I don't know how my neck holds
my head up – it's so big like a melon. I don't think we're
designed to see ourselves from the back, I really don't. I was
like a small village.

I just hadn't expected to see it, you know what I mean, and it just cut the day in half – I was having a really good day and then I saw that video and the day was ruined. The video was a precipice moment. Shouldn't have watched it.

My fridge and I have a complicated relationship. Fridge and I are having an affair. I see it when I'm feeling lonely or like crap or bored but I know it will never give me what I want. Fridge is always up for it and doesn't seem to want it to end so I can see it whenever I like. The longer I spend there, my face bathed in fridge's soothing light, the more involved I become. I get hungrier and hungrier.

Maybe I'll get a big hard hammer and bring it down on my fridge in the middle of the night. This is just what I needed, wasn't it, to motivate me into change, and all the experts say that you only have to make small lifestyle changes every day to see progress … this was just the motivation I needed …

Except – well, except … it's just that …

Well, when has shame and self-loathing ever ever helped me or encouraged me to take action about anything ever!?
It won't help me now. If I'm going to get healthier, if I'm going to call it off with Fridge, well, then, I can't be shamed into it.

The other day, I accidentally caught sight of my full nakedness in the bathroom mirror and, for a few moments, I thought I looked magnificent, but then it also made me jump a bit because I thought my pubes were a spider.